# 75 Gifts of Advice for the Christian Graduate

—•—

That Your Future Self Will Appreciate

KLO Publishing, LLC

## Kelly L. Owens

Copyright © 2023 by Kelly L. Owens

All rights reserved.

No portion of this book may be reproduced in any form without written permission from the publisher or author, except as permitted by U.S. copyright law.

This publication is designed to provide accurate and authoritative information in regard to the subject matter covered. It is sold with the understanding that neither the author nor the publisher is engaged in rendering legal, investment, accounting, or other professional services. While the publisher and author have used their best efforts in preparing this book, they make no representations or warranties with respect to the accuracy or completeness of the contents of this book and specifically disclaim any implied warranties of merchantability or fitness for a particular purpose. No warranty may be created or extended by sales representatives or written sales materials. The advice and strategies contained herein may not be suitable for your situation. You should consult with a professional when appropriate. Neither the publisher nor the author shall be liable for any loss of profit or any other commercial damages, including but not limited to special, incidental, consequential, personal, or other damages.

All Scripture quotations, unless otherwise indicated, are taken from The Holy Bible, English Standard Version. Copyright ©2001 by http://www.crosswaybibles.org/, a publishing ministry of Good News Publishers.

Book Cover by Allen Owens

ISBN: 979-8-9880051-0-0 (Paperback)

ISBN: 979-8-9880051-1-7 (E-book)

For my family with all my love

*With love for my baby Mikaela on her graduation day! So proud of my Zoologist!*

*Mom* ♥

# **Contents**

| | | |
|---|---|---|
| Introduction | | 1 |
| 1. | Actions Speak Loudly | 3 |
| 2. | Always Be Trustworthy | 5 |
| 3. | Always Be Yourself | 7 |
| 4. | Ask For Help | 9 |
| 5. | Assume Noble Intent | 11 |
| 6. | Attitude of Gratitude | 13 |
| 7. | Attitude Determines Altitude | 15 |
| 8. | Be On Time | 17 |
| 9. | Believe In Yourself | 19 |
| 10. | Better Not Bitter | 21 |
| 11. | Build Social Capital | 23 |
| 12. | Build Your Circle | 25 |
| 13. | Build Your Relationships | 27 |
| 14. | Change Your World | 29 |
| 15. | Cherish Your Elders | 31 |
| 16. | Commit To Growth | 33 |
| 17. | Connect With Others | 35 |

| | | |
|---|---|---|
| 18. | Create a Budget | 37 |
| 19. | Do It Anyway | 39 |
| 20. | Do It Now | 41 |
| 21. | Eat Healthy Foods | 43 |
| 22. | Express Your Emotions | 45 |
| 23. | Failing is OK | 47 |
| 24. | Find A Mentor | 49 |
| 25. | Find Joy Daily | 51 |
| 26. | Find Your Passion | 53 |
| 27. | Follow Your Dreams | 55 |
| 28. | Get In Nature | 57 |
| 29. | Get Your Exercise | 59 |
| 30. | Get Your Sleep | 61 |
| 31. | Give Your Best | 63 |
| 32. | Go to Church | 65 |
| 33. | Good Stewardship Matters | 67 |
| 34. | Guard Your Thoughts | 69 |
| 35. | Hold Your Ground | 71 |
| 36. | Invest In Yourself | 73 |
| 37. | Keep Being Curious | 75 |
| 38. | Keep Things Simple | 77 |
| 39. | Know Your Boundaries | 79 |
| 40. | Know Your Non-Negotiables | 81 |
| 41. | Know Your Values | 83 |

| | | |
|---|---|---|
| 42. | Knowing the One | 85 |
| 43. | Know Your Why | 87 |
| 44. | Learn About Resilience | 89 |
| 45. | Learn Goal Setting | 91 |
| 46. | Learn Home Basics | 93 |
| 47. | Learn to Communicate | 95 |
| 48. | Learn to Forgive | 97 |
| 49. | Learn to Influence | 99 |
| 50. | Let God Lead | 101 |
| 51. | Limit Credit Cards | 103 |
| 52. | Live Below Means | 105 |
| 53. | Live By Faith | 107 |
| 54. | Live In Balance | 109 |
| 55. | Make Your Bed | 111 |
| 56. | Manage Your Perspective | 113 |
| 57. | Manage Your Stress | 115 |
| 58. | Never Tolerate Disrespect | 117 |
| 59. | No More Drama | 119 |
| 60. | Offer Some Help | 121 |
| 61. | Organize Your Documents | 123 |
| 62. | Own Your Mistakes | 125 |
| 63. | Plan to Succeed | 127 |
| 64. | Plan To Tithe | 129 |
| 65. | Prioritize Not Multitask | 131 |

| 66. | Progress Not Perfection | 133 |
| --- | --- | --- |
| 67. | Read Good Books | 135 |
| 68. | Release Dead Weight | 137 |
| 69. | Save Some Money | 139 |
| 70. | Specialize in Something | 141 |
| 71. | Time is Valuable | 143 |
| 72. | Travel the World | 145 |
| 73. | Trust Your Gut | 147 |
| 74. | You Are Enough | 149 |
| 75. | You Deserve Better | 151 |
| About Author | | 153 |

# Introduction

This book was inspired by a question posed on Facebook. The question was, what advice would you give your 18-year-old self using only three words? Of course, I had a few, but then I started thinking about what I would tell myself if I had the opportunity to go back in time.

I found myself making a list of all the three-word phrases of advice I would tell myself. Before I knew it, I had seventy-five of them. Being a Christian, I could easily see where what I was advising my younger self was backed up by scripture. In this book, I included the scriptures I believe represent the foundation of the advice given. Of course, there were more I could have used, and I encourage you to seek out those verses.

This is not an exhaustive list by any means, and as time goes on, you may find what you would add to the list. Have conversations with your loved ones about how they would personally implement the advice. I hope this book sparks meaningful conversations with your loved ones and other respected leaders or mentors in your life.

Remember, life is an adventure. There will be times of joy, anticipation, fear, frustration, grief, and bravery. May you seek God first in all that you do, as He provides the wisest counsel. Trust in him. He will guide you on the correct path and shine light upon it to help you see.

·····●··●·····

# 1

## Actions Speak Loudly

> Little children, let us not love in word or talk but in deed and in truth
>
> 1 John 3:18

You have heard the phrase actions speak louder than words. This is because words can be lip service, but the actions of others tell you what is true. It can tell you what they really think, believe, feel, and are willing to do or not do. When others show you the truth through their actions, take note. That is not to say people cannot make mistakes and never deserve a second chance. However, repeated actions tell you that the person is not willing to change. They may say they are sorry, but if they keep repeating an action, it is evidence of their lack of remorse. They are feeling sorry they were caught. They are not truly wanting to make things right.

Additionally, think about what your actions tell others about you. Are you being inconsistent between what you say and what you do? Others are noticing if you are being inconsistent. They may not say anything to you about it, but they are noticing. Broken promises are a significant way we can be inconsistent. Not following through on what you say you will do is a way to show that inconsistency. The bottom line is that our actions tell others if we are trustworthy or not.

People who are not trustworthy are not given opportunities for advancement in careers, in relationships, and keep themselves stuck in life generally. By not learning this valuable lesson, they continue to wonder why things do not work out for them or make excuses about the lack of opportunities in life. They have not figured out that they are the root cause themselves by showing others they are untrustworthy.

·····•··•····

## 2

## ALWAYS BE TRUSTWORTHY

One who is faithful in a very little is also faithful in much, and one who is dishonest in a very little is also dishonest in much.

Luke 16:10

As shared in the prior wisdom, being trustworthy gives you greater access to the meaningful things in life. When we are trustworthy, others want to have us around. No one wants a friend they cannot trust. No boss wants an employee he or she cannot trust. No boyfriend or girlfriend wants to build a relationship with a person he or she cannot trust.

When we can be trusted with small things, others will begin to trust us with bigger and more important things. If you fail to be trusted in the small things, you show others they cannot count on you. Always do the right thing even when no one is watching. One, you may think no one is watching, but they might be. Two, doing the right thing when no one is watching is building character. You need to be in the habit of doing what is right no matter if being watched or not. It must be a muscle you build and instinctively do to show the world you are trustworthy.

Being trustworthy means keeping promises. Being trustworthy means telling the truth. Being trustworthy means being a good steward of what is given to you or borrowed by you. If you borrow something, treat it well and return it on time. If you are given a gift, taking care of it shows you appreciate it. Others are willing to give more to you if you care for what you have already been given. No one wants to give to a person who treats things poorly because it can be not only a waste of their money but also their time. No one wants to give opportunities to someone who will squander them.

## 3

## ALWAYS BE YOURSELF

Do your best to present yourself to God as one approved, a worker who has no need to be ashamed, rightly handling the word of truth.

2 Timothy 2:15

You were created to be uniquely yourself. As you get older, you learn to accept yourself more than you probably did when you were younger. When we are kids in school, we have to deal with a lot of peer pressure and live up to what we think will get us accepted. We often become chameleons in a crowd just to be sure we fit in.

Rejection is a scary and hurtful thing. However, there is no avoiding it in life. Not everyone is going to be part of your group or click with you. That is ok. As I have gotten older, I have learned to find my tribe. Those are people who value what I value. We match up on life goals, what we do for fun, and what we find inspiring about each other. We just click. Even if you feel like it is hard to show your real, true self to others, practice doing that a little bit at a time. You will find those who support you and accept you just the way you are.

The last thing you want to do is go through life always feeling like you have to wear a mask to fit in with a certain group. Social networks can be where you are celebrated for being you or very discouraging because of the norms set up that do not allow for individuality.

··•·•••·••··

## 4

## Ask For Help

If any of you lacks wisdom, let him ask God, who gives generously to all without reproach, and it will be given him

James 1:5

One thing life will teach you is that there will be moments you will get in over your head. It happens to all of us at some point. You have a choice to either ask for help or to continue to be in over your head. When we choose to continue thinking we have all the answers, we can dig a deeper hole. Arrogance and ignorance are a bad combination. It is easy to think we have all the answers. I know I was a bit of a know-it-all in my younger years. The arrogance of my youth and my lack of experience making me ignorant did not always lead to desirable outcomes. As time went on, I quickly began to learn that others may just have some good advice because they had the wisdom of experience.

Not long ago, we had a young employee who had great potential, but we began to notice that he would not ask for help until he had wasted several days not getting a task completed as expected. We thought he was working on things but when the task deadline arrived, that is when he finally would admit he did not understand what was being asked of him or that he was not sure how to complete the task. Despite being reminded more than once that it was ok to ask for help, he continued in this pattern. Ultimately, we had to let him go. His refusal to ask for help and be open to learning from the more experienced coworkers showed us a pattern that was not going to be acceptable on the job. It is better to ask for help than to waste precious time and let problems grow into bigger situations.

······

# 5

## Assume Noble Intent

Do not judge by appearances, but judge with right judgment.

John 7:24

One of my mentors shares this with every person he coaches and mentors. What this means is to not jump to conclusions and assume the worst about someone else's intentions in a situation. You may not like what the other person said or did, but do you really know their intentions to pass judgment on it? When we jump to conclusions about why someone did or said something we did not like, we are mind-reading. None of us were born with that gift. We assign our thoughts to their actions. We state it as though it were a fact and then we feel angry at the other person. We may even go so far as to state this "fact" to others and trash-talk about the other person.

When we assume noble intent, we actively practice thinking that the other person did what they did for good reasons known maybe only to them. We assume they did not do things on purpose to cause problems for others or to frustrate them. This is about everyday situations that can cause irritation. I am not talking about those who abuse others. That is a different case.

By assuming noble intent, we reduce the frustration that we feel and we do not engage in petty gossip with others. We can reduce the likelihood of letting things go so far that we see the other person as our enemy. Keep in mind that you will say and do things that you believe you had a good reason for it. Would you want others to assume the worst or would you want them to assume noble intent about you? This goes both ways. You have to give what you want to receive.

# 6

## ATTITUDE OF GRATITUDE

*In every way and everywhere we accept this with all gratitude.*

Acts 24:3

This one will help you have a joyful life. Not having an attitude of gratitude can lead to a life of self-inflicted misery. Have you ever met people who were always complaining? The complainers in life just cannot see the positive or the good in anything. They constantly focus on what they do not have or that things were not exactly as they wanted them to be. We can see poor people filled with joy and rich people filled with misery.

Having an attitude of gratitude can help get you through challenging times. It is easy to wallow in misery when you refuse to look for any kind of silver lining or at least one thing you can be grateful for that day. You will have hard times in life. Everyone does. The people who believe their life is generally happy are those who have mastered the attitude of gratitude. Those who grumble constantly about small things are those who refuse to look for anything to be grateful about. It can be something as simple as being grateful for a day of pleasant weather. Practice finding at least three things you can be grateful for to help build resilience. When you have resilience, you are better equipped to deal with the challenges that life will throw your way.

There was a time in my life that I was a single mom, working full time, and having all the house and yard work to do. I was having a pity party one day about never having any downtime. I was tired but still needed to go mow the yard. As I was mowing, it occurred to me that other single moms living in apartments would give their right arm for their children to have their own yard to play in. At that moment, I became filled with so much gratitude that I had the house and the yard. I never whined again about having to mow that yard!

···•••·•••··

# 7

## ATTITUDE DETERMINES ALTITUDE

> For to set the mind on the flesh is death, but to set the mind on the Spirit is life and peace.
>
> Romans 8:6

I have always loved this saying. How far and how high you go in life is determined by your attitude. The right kind of attitude opens doors. The right kind of attitude gets you invited into circles of successful people. Successful people do not spend time with unsuccessful people. Unsuccessful people have "stinking thinking". They believe they are victims of circumstances and are full of excuses as to why they cannot make any changes. They have a million reasons why they are stuck in life and it is never because of their lack of willingness to learn new things, put forth an effort, and make sacrifices.

Have a mindset that anything worth having is going to take effort and sacrifice. Getting to the higher altitudes in life means having the willingness to learn new things, temporarily making sacrifices of time and money to get access to the training needed, and getting rid of excuses. Those who rise to higher altitudes accept personal responsibility for getting themselves there. It is all about having the right kind of attitude to know that you have to be the one to do the work. Nothing gets handed to you and you are not entitled to anything that you did not work to get.

Entitled, spoiled attitudes will keep you stuck. The real world will not give you anything just because you think it should. The real world will pass you by. You have to get in the game and off the sidelines. You need to check your attitude and develop the kind of mindset that will reap rewards and benefits. If you have not had people in your life model this for you, look around until you find these kinds of people so you can learn what it is that they do. Success leaves clues. Find out how they think and what sets them apart. Model your thinking after theirs.

·····•••·•••··

# 8

## BE ON TIME

Making the best use of the time, because the days are evil.

Ephesians 5:16

Being on time shows respect for others. When times are set for dinners, get-togethers, appointments, and events, that means others are waiting on you. When you repeatedly show up late, you give others the message that you do not value them or their time.

We all know that person that others expect to show up late because they are simply known for never being on time. Some of the busiest people in the world can show up on time for things, while those who do not have pressing commitments show up late all the time. Those who are late get in the habit of being late. They do not give any thought to how long it may take to drive somewhere, get things gathered for what may be needed at the time set with others, or even simply find their car keys.

Successful people show up on time. They make the effort to value others' time and their own. Can you imagine if a busy person showed up late to their first meeting? The rest of their day is thrown off because it pushes all appointments back or something has to be rescheduled. Valuing your own time matters too.

The trick to being on time is to plan ahead. Get things organized and gathered the night before if you have an early morning appointment. Set your clock earlier so you get started with plenty of time to get ready and drive to where you need to be. If you want to stop for a coffee or scroll through social media, that is fine, but schedule the time to do that. Do not cram it in an already tight schedule, then make others wait on you. Being late to work matters and many have been fired for habitually being late. Get in the habit of being on time and showing others you value them and their time.

··•••••···

## 9

## BELIEVE IN YOURSELF

For you formed my inward parts; you knitted me together in my mother's womb. I praise you, for I am fearfully and wonderfully made. Wonderful are your works; my soul knows it very well.

Psalm 139:13-14

So many people take their dreams to their graves because they simply do not believe in themselves enough. They spend their lives focusing on what they think they are not instead of recognizing who they are and what they bring to the table. Each of us was born with innate gifts that just need to be nurtured and built upon.

It is easy to believe you are not capable of achieving your big dreams when you focus solely on the times that you did not do so well at something. We all are lousy at something, but we are also very gifted with other things. I cannot sing. Well, I can, but no one wants to hear that. I was not gifted with a singing voice. If I spent my life focusing on the memory of my choir teacher making that awful face while I was auditioning, I would not have gotten out of my comfort zone to try other things. I could have turned that embarrassing moment into something way bigger than it was and counted myself out of a lot of opportunities for fear of embarrassment again.

I had to learn what I was gifted with and pursue dreams that were in alignment with those gifts. Some gifts you may not see as being that big of a deal, but you never know what those talents could lead to in the future. You were born for a purpose and you have to believe in yourself enough to step into that purpose. As time goes on, you will figure out your talents and strengths. Spend time nurturing those because they will lead to greater things in your life. Do not spend excessive time focusing on what you think you are not and comparing yourself to others. That is like watering weeds. You want to water the flowers instead.

··· •• · • • ···

## 10

## BETTER NOT BITTER

Let all bitterness and wrath and anger and clamor and slander be put away from you, along with all malice.

Ephesians 4:31

This is one of my favorites because it led me out of a very dark time in my life. I am so grateful I embraced this bit of wisdom because it has served me well. I remember the day I decided I would be better and not bitter when I was going through a divorce.

I knew I did not want to be one of those bitter people who spent all their time talking about their ex-spouse and all the wrongs that were inflicted upon them. That was not the kind of life I wanted to have. Things did not turn out as I had envisioned, but that did not mean I had to wallow in self-pity and bitterness. If I had to GO through this dark time in my life, I might as well GROW through it. I would strive to become a better version of myself, learn lessons from that experience, and build a new life that was filled with joy and purpose.

I can say after having gone through that dark time of my life, that I did become a better version of myself. I learned to trust in God more, to have more gratitude, to find joy in the small moments each day, and to develop skills I had previously never tried to use before. I ended up being a happier person when it was all said and done. I was not bitter. I was at peace and enjoying life.

## 11

## BUILD SOCIAL CAPITAL

Two are better than one, because they have a good reward for their toil. **10** For if they fall, one will lift up his fellow. But woe to him who is alone when he falls and has not another to lift him up!

Ecclesiastes 4:9-10

This idea may not be one you have heard before. We hear about having financial capital, working capital in businesses, human capital, and so forth. When we build social capital, we are building connections that can help us possibly have access to resources. We can also be a resource to someone else when they need it as well.

This is more than networking and rubbing elbows with the elite in our community. This is about having shared values and mutual service to one another. Social engagement helps to bring diverse people together for a common goal. Nonprofit volunteerism is an excellent example of this. People work together for a shared value within the mission of that organization. These diverse individuals may never have met each other if not for this engagement. When people get to know each other based on common ground, the differences between them seem to diminish. However, diversity can be of great value too.

As we go through life, there are times when we need to ask ourselves who we know within our wider social circle who may be able to help with specialized situations. The more effort you make to build your social capital, the easier it is to find someone within your network who might be a resource. There is an old saying that it is all in who you know. There is truth in that. The beauty of this is that you also become a person that others think of when they have a particular need you are especially skilled. This is how people succeed in business and their communities.

··· •• •• •••

## 12

## Build Your Circle

> Whoever walks with the wise becomes wise, but the companion of fools will suffer harm.
>
> Proverbs 13:20

This one may sound like the previous one, but it is different. I have often heard within the personal development field that the five people we spend the most time with have the most influence on us. You will want those five people to encourage you to be your best.

You may have family members who are not supportive and struggling with their issues. You can still be family, but you need to reduce the level of influence they have on you. The same with some friends. As time goes on, you may need to spend less time with certain people and make more time for the ones who have a positive influence on you.

Be selective about who your influential people will be. You do not want the perpetually unemployed cousin giving you advice about your career. You do not want a friend who has never owned a business telling you all the reasons why you should not start your own. Be aware that you may have family and friends who fear you leaving them behind if you pursue additional training, go for that new job, open your own business, or pursue a new creative outlet. Just because they are too afraid to pursue these things for themselves, they will want to hold you back too. They will talk so much about why things will not work out; you will begin to doubt yourself. Select your circle carefully.

··•••·•••··

## 13

# BUILD YOUR RELATIONSHIPS

> Above all, keep loving one another earnestly, since love covers a multitude of sins.
>
> 1 Peter 4:8

Sadly, many do not realize what they have until it is gone. If we do not value and invest time in those we care about, we may find them no longer a part of our lives. Just like a plant, the ones you water stay green and growing, and the ones you do not turn brown and wither away.

Life will get busy. It will take effort to keep all the demands of daily life from taking over the time that should belong to building your relationships. As you get married and have children, you will find that you will have to make choices to allow you to keep your family as a priority. The messages you get from this world tell you that you have to constantly hustle, and if you do not post on social media for a few hours, you will not be relevant. There is a place and time for everything. You do not want the ones you care deeply about to feel they have to compete for your attention with everything else.

When you spend time with someone, put down your phone and listen to them. Be present and in the moment with them. Avoid being distracted by other things during the time you promised to be with them. When others feel less important than all the distractions, they will begin to pull away. They will begin to spend their time with others who make them feel appreciated for just being who they are. No one wants to fight for your attention. If it happens often enough, eventually they will walk away.

··•••••••··

## 14

# CHANGE YOUR WORLD

> Do not be conformed to this world, but be transformed by the renewal of your mind, that by testing you may discern what is the will of God, what is good and acceptable and perfect.
>
> Romans 12:2

You may think this is a bit overwhelming when you read it. It is not about you carrying the weight of the world on your shoulders or trying to address global issues. It is about identifying what is within your daily world. Who is in your immediate realm of existence? This could be your group of friends. It could be at your job. It could be in one of your classes at school. Wherever you are at this moment is your world.

You can influence something positive or negative within your world. It is purely your choice what you do within that world. You can show kindness to another. You can help solve a problem. You can pick up the trash left behind by someone else. There is a popular phrase about being the change you want to see in the world. If you do not like what you see, change starts with you. Become a shining example of what you would like to see others do in the world.

We can offer our opinions all day long with little to no effect. Actively being and doing the things that lead to change in your world does have an effect.

## 15

## CHERISH YOUR ELDERS

Let the elders who rule well be considered worthy of double honor, especially those who labor in preaching and teaching.

1 Timothy 5:17

So many of us have wished we could go back and talk with a loved one who is now gone. While your elderly loved one is still with you, please take the time to see them. Let them tell you stories of when they were younger. Ask them questions about what they believe have been the most important lessons they have learned.

I am so glad I spent time with my grandmother before she passed away. I wrote down all her information in a notebook. I have always remembered that day and learned things about her that I did not know before. If there is time, give your loved one a memory book and ask them to write down their memories. You will treasure this book after they are gone.

You may not have an elderly loved one in your family. Instead, pick someone you are close with and learn more about him or her. You will not regret the time taken to do this and you will probably learn things you never knew. We are not born old. We all have a lifetime of memories of when we were younger. We are different people throughout our life stages. Learning about your loved one as they were in different stages of their life is so rewarding. You will see them in a new light.

·········

## 16

## COMMIT TO GROWTH

Your word is a lamp to my feet and a light to my path.

Psalm 119:105

Make a commitment to growth and have a mindset of self-development. I have witnessed many times in my life the value of being committed to growth. I have also witnessed the detrimental impact of not valuing it. Just because you have graduated does not mean you stop learning.

To build a career, you will have to learn new skills that may require your participation in a training program. If you do not want to make the sacrifice of time on that now, later you may find yourself being passed over for promotions or having difficulty getting a job offer with better pay. As mentioned before, life will get busy and you will have to make choices about how you spend time. Consider the opportunities that investing in your personal growth will allow you to gain. Think about the potential lost opportunities that may occur if you choose to pass up the investment.

Growth can also be about your personal life and spiritual life. It can be about finding purpose and meaning. It can be about growing in your relationship with Christ and in your Christian walk. Stagnation leads to boredom. Staying active in learning new things and growing yourself will improve your quality of life.

············

## 17

# CONNECT WITH OTHERS

Do nothing from selfish ambition or conceit, but in humility count others more significant than yourselves. Let each of you look not only to his own interests, but also to the interests of others.

Philippians 2:3-4

The art of connection will prove to be invaluable to you in just about every area of your life. Your ability to connect will have a positive impact on your relationships with family members, love interests, friends, coworkers, bosses, community members, and so on.

Believe it or not, your ability to connect with strangers can help you in customer service situations whether you are the customer or the employee working to help another. It will increase the likelihood of another being willing to help you. Being rude, dismissive, and demanding does not make others want to help you in the least.

Seeing others as valuable is the foundation for connecting. If you do not see others as worthy of your effort, you will not successfully connect. People instantly feel what is genuine and what is superficial. Once you see others as having value, you then respectfully approach them. After that, take a moment to be friendly and ask how their day is going. It is amazing how many walls come down by doing something as simple as that. If you want to deepen the connection, you begin to ask questions to genuinely learn about the other person. Connection is an art that can be mastered.

## 18

## CREATE A BUDGET

The plans of the diligent lead surely to abundance, but everyone who is hasty comes only to poverty.

Proverbs 21:5

If you want to avoid financial troubles, learn how to create a budget and stick to it. A budget is more than just a tool to tell to help you manage spending money on what you need. It can also aid you in getting what you want. Knowing the difference between needs and wants will be crucial to your budget as well. Groceries are a need and cable tv is a want.

Base your budget on take-home pay. Never base it on your salary because taxes, insurance, and other costs come out of your paycheck, such as when you invest in a 401K or optional insurance coverage beyond what your company provides. Learn the appropriate percentages of your pay to spend on housing and transportation. Overspending in a key area leaves little in other areas.

Basic budgeting is a fundamental skill that will lead to financial success in life. It will serve you well by helping you protect your credit score, avoid bankruptcy, save for the dream vacation, or buy your first home. You may have never been taught how to budget, but you can easily learn this by doing an internet search for videos on how to do it. Have the right mindset about budgets. A budget is your ally in helping you find the finances for what you want in life.

## 19

## DO IT ANYWAY

*Fear not, for I am with you; be not dismayed, for I am your God; I will strengthen you, I will help you, I will uphold you with my righteous right hand.*

Isaiah 41:10

This bit of advice does not mean to do whatever you feel like despite the laws, the warnings from trusted people, or to help yourself to something you did not earn. No, this gift of wisdom is about getting past your fears and pushing yourself beyond self-imposed limitations. It is about feeling fear and doing it anyway.

I know that putting yourself out there is scary because of possible criticism and embarrassment. However, the life you want is on the other side of fear. It is outside your comfort zone. You will find life is full of opportunities when you are open to them. Those who create a small comfort zone will never see the resources and options available to them. In many cases, the solution is outside our comfort zone. I am sure you have met people who *"have a problem for every solution"*. They find every reason to dismiss possible solutions. They are too afraid to try those options because they never step out of their comfort zone.

Stretching ourselves through courageous actions leads to rewards. The beauty of stretching is that we cannot get back to the way we were beforehand. We are forever changed and in a positive way. Practicing this wisdom will grow you beyond your small comfort zone. You will stop worrying about what others think and will learn that even if you fail, you still win. You win because you grew.

·····•··•·····

## 20

# Do It Now

Do not boast about tomorrow, for you do not know what a day may bring.

Proverbs 27:1

I have a mentor who says to himself repeatedly, "do it now", "do it now", "do it now". He does this for things he knows are important and can be easily addressed right now. There is no need for him to procrastinate and do it later. All that does is add to his to-do list. He knows it is in his nature to want to put things off. He has learned over the years that the small things put off until later pile up. They become more of a challenge because they have now become urgent. This is because he waited. He is now faced with trying to meet a deadline while juggling even more things that require his attention.

I am sure you can think of times when you have put things off and later regretted the procrastination. Procrastination becomes a habit.

However, Do-It-Now can become a habit too. If you can complete a task that takes less than thirty minutes and nothing else is a higher priority at the moment, then do it now.

The Do It Now mentality can serve you well by not letting things grow into bigger issues. There is a cost to procrastination. The first cost is higher stress levels. When you put off things, eventually time will run out and you have to rush to meet a deadline. It may allow a small problem to grow into a bigger problem too. That may cost you more time and money to solve the problem.

## 21

## EAT HEALTHY FOODS

If you have found honey, eat only enough for you, lest you have your fill of it and vomit it.

Proverbs 25:16

Having a habit of eating healthy food each day when you are young will pay off more than you realize. At this point in your life, you may find it easy to eat junk food without any impact. However, habits have a cumulative effect on our lives. They can lead to rewards or they can lead to regrets.

Build the habits now that your future self will thank you for one day. The habit of eating high-fat and high-sugar foods will lead to unhealthy weight gain, food cravings that are hard to control, and eventually high cholesterol and other weight-related diseases. Then when that happens, we have the challenge of trying to reverse those conditions. We have to work hard to develop the habit of healthy eating because we have programmed ourselves to eat junk instead.

By starting young and being aware of your habits, you will gain so many benefits as you age. You will look younger than your age, you will still be active doing the things you enjoyed in your younger years, you will not have to fight weight-related illnesses, and generally feel well. Aging happens to everyone. You have control over some aspects of it. It is your choice if you have rewards or regrets.

## 22

## EXPRESS YOUR EMOTIONS

*Be angry and do not sin; do not let the sun go down on your anger,*

Ephesians 4:26

Our world is constantly telling us to put on our game face and suck it up. There are times when this is a reality and is needed once in a while. Certain situations call for being logical and doing the task at hand because of the seriousness of what is going on. However, you are not a robot and cannot pretend you never feel. This is about finding a balance.

Some people are strongly driven by their emotions to the point they behave impulsively. They lash out at others inappropriately. Others bury their emotions with food, drugs, sex, and workaholism. The key is about a healthy expression of your emotions so that you are not going to extremes. Having a safe place to share your feelings will be important as you navigate life. You will encounter times of hardship and will need to know how to deal with the emotions as you make your way through the situation.

Begin to build a group of friends with whom you are safe to share your feelings without fear of ridicule or judgment. Develop the habit of journaling to dump out everything in your head and what is on your heart. Sometimes emotions can be confusing. If we keep them bottled up inside, they continue to cause confusion. Expressing them helps to make sense of them. It also helps us to step back and think more clearly before we take action.

## 23

# FAILING IS OK

My flesh and my heart may fail, but God is the strength of my heart and my portion forever.

Psalm 73:26

This one is a particular favorite of mine. As I have invested time in my personal growth, mentors have told me to fail fast and fail often. What that means is to get out there and try out my ideas. I will learn what works and what does not work. I will never have that information if I stay stuck thinking about what I am going to do instead of implementing it. Failing is a form of learning. It is simply information about what does not work. It is not a reflection of who you are as a person.

Many become concerned with the idea of failing and wondering what others will think. They fear the opinions of others. Once you understand what failing truly means, it will not have power over you any longer. As I got older, I let go of the fear of what others may think. I decided that other people's opinions do not pay my bills. At one point, I knew I needed a path for advancement. I saw an opportunity that appeared financially risky. However, I decided to bet on myself and went for it. It turned out just fine. Not everything I tried was a glowing success. However, the failures were not the end of the world either.

Failure is just feedback. That is all it is. You learn from it and become wiser. Successful people have failed many times. They are not the overnight success you may think. There was a lot of trial and error before they made it.

## 24

## FIND A MENTOR

> Without counsel plans fail, but with many advisers they succeed.
>
> Proverbs 15:22

One of the actions I wish had taken sooner in life was finding a mentor. I did not understand the value of having someone who had already accomplished the goals I was setting for myself to guide me along the way. Can you imagine how learning from someone who had "been there, done that" would have saved me from doing things the hard way?

Mentors are people who have the experience to share information with you that can help guide you on the right path sooner. They can provide clarity when there is confusion. They are a sounding board to hear your ideas and ask you important questions that you need to consider as you make your decisions. Mentors are not just there to tell you what to do. Good mentors can help you think for yourself in ways you may not have developed without their influence. My thinking changed once I had mentors share their nuggets of wisdom. I considered things from a more experienced point of view through their guidance. I could not have done that on my own. I did not have the experience yet to have that point of view.

Take time to think about where you are heading with your goals, then look around for people who are ahead of you in achieving those goals. Many people are happy to mentor others. Do not be afraid to share your goals with this person and ask him or her if they would be willing to mentor you. For now, use this book as a mentor. There are other great books written by people you can consider a mentor too. Not all mentors have to be in person. Be open to mentoring in a variety of ways.

## 25

# FIND JOY DAILY

A joyful heart is good medicine, but a crushed spirit dries up the bones.

Proverbs 17:22

Have you ever met people that constantly complained or found something wrong at every moment? They have no joy in their lives. Their view of the world is pessimistic and they search out things to be disappointed about. You can train your mind to always notice the negative or you can train your mind to notice the positive. You actually can create neural pathways that support whatever it is you spend your time focusing on. Look up the research on that if you do not believe me.

Train your mind to find joy each day. This is taking time to notice something beautiful. It is noticing the kindness of others. It is seeing the silver lining in challenging situations. It is also actively choosing to participate in activities you have fun doing. If you never make time to do what you enjoy, the next thing you find happening is being in a grind of going to work, watching tv for a while, going to bed, and starting it all over again the next day. That becomes monotonous.

Plan something fun to look forward to at least once a week, while practicing seeing the positive in each day. If you do this, you will become a happier person. You will not become like that person who always sees something wrong in every situation.

## 26

## FIND YOUR PASSION

> For I know the plans I have for you, declares the Lord, plans for welfare and not for evil, to give you a future and a hope.
>
> Jeremiah 29:11

This one can be challenging. Many are in their later years and still have not figured out what is their passion. My mentor, John C. Maxwell, taught me to ask three questions. What makes you sing? What makes you cry? What do you dream about?

When he refers to what makes you sing, he is wanting you to identify what fills your heart with joy. Begin to journal the things that you find bring you great joy. If you volunteer or do a specific job, what parts of that do you enjoy? When he asks what makes you cry, he is wanting you to think about the things that break your heart. This gives you an indication of the things you care deeply about. For example, you may watch the news and see the devastation that recent storms left behind. If that touches you deeply, then disaster relief may be an area that means something to you.

The next question is discovering what you dream about. Ask yourself what you would do if you absolutely knew you could not fail. Money and time are not a problem. Access to resources is not a problem. Education and skills are not a problem. What would it be?

Look at your answers to these questions. How can the three come together? The union of those three is where your passion can be found.

·· • •• • •• ···

## 27

## FOLLOW YOUR DREAMS

> And we know that for those who love God all things work together for good, for those who are called according to his purpose
>
> Romans 8:28

The thing most people regret in life is what they did not do vs. what they did. They regret the missed opportunities because they were too afraid to say yes. They listened to the people around them who imposed their fears by telling them all the reasons they should not pursue their dreams. You cannot afford to let the fears others have become your own.

This is why building your circle with people who are pursuing their dreams, and who are supportive of you pursuing your dreams, matters so much. If you surround yourself with people who can never see an opportunity, have a problem for every solution, and refuse to leave their comfort zones, you will find yourself doing the same.

If you are excited about the possibility of pursuing what you dream about, take some time to list out ways to get it. List out what you need to learn about. Determine what resources you might need. Develop a plan for how you will get the information you need and who might be able to connect you to resources. You live in a time where access to information is unbelievably easy to obtain, and often for free. Spend time thinking about what can go right instead of what can go wrong. As you begin to follow your dreams, new things will be revealed to you and that dream may shift into a slightly different version of it. That is ok. You may find you want to pursue a different dream altogether. Again, that is ok. The key here is to be pursuing your dreams and allowing yourself the opportunity to grow.

·· · • • · • • · ··

## 28

## GET IN NATURE

For you shall go out in joy and be led forth in peace; the mountains and the hills before you shall break forth into singing, and all the trees of the field shall clap their hands.

Isaiah 55:12

We live in a world of artificial light, manmade materials, technology, artificial intelligence, and virtual reality. All of that serves a purpose and can be useful. However, there is so much benefit in getting unplugged and into nature. Our lives are filled with stressful demands and we are exposed to all kinds of electrical charges from the technology around us.

Simply getting barefoot and standing on the earth, whether it is grass, sand, or dirt, has been shown to cause grounding. Being grounded means connecting with the earth. Scientists have begun to study the beneficial effects of grounding and reducing stress. What they are finding is that excess electrical charges in our bodies go back into the earth when we stand barefoot. This reduces inflammation. Inflammation is a root cause of many health concerns.

Grounding can help calm your nervous system. So, when you feel your stress levels rising, make time each day to get barefoot outside. This is a simple way to develop a habit for good health. Your future self will thank you.

······ ·· ···

## 29

## GET YOUR EXERCISE

> Or do you not know that your body is a temple of the Holy Spirit within you, whom you have from God? You are not your own, for you were bought with a price. So glorify God in your body.
>
> 1 Corinthians 6:19-20

Once again, the world we live in leads to being sedentary. We have so many conveniences that we are not using our bodies as much as our ancestors did. They had to walk to get places. They did more manual labor as well. They got up early, physically challenged their bodies all day long, then rested when the sun went down.

Today we use elevators instead of walking the stairs. We use our cars to drive a mile down the road. Unfortunately, many of our cities and towns are not pedestrian friendly. Everything is designed for us to drive our cars everywhere. Because of that, we have to make the effort to get exercise. Simply walking has many benefits. It improves our mental health, boosts immunity, supports weight loss, improves heart health, and increases mobility. As we age, mobility declines if we do not proactively do something about it.

Getting in the habit early in your life will pay off. You can avoid the health issues related to being sedentary. They say that being sedentary is the new form of smoking. This means that being sedentary is causing many of the health problems we see, just like the health problems seen by smoking. It is a known factor for causing a decline in health.

# 30

## GET YOUR SLEEP

And he said to them, "Come away by yourselves to a desolate place and rest a while." For many were coming and going, and they had no leisure even to eat.

Mark 6:31

Many do not get the sleep they need in our modern society. It was a problem before smartphones, but it is even more so now that they exist. The blue light emitted off our televisions, computer screens, and phones actually can disturb our production of melatonin. Melatonin is a hormone known to help with the ability to fall asleep and stay asleep.

When we do not get enough sleep on a continuous basis, it begins to affect our ability to think clearly and manage our emotions. When we are not operating at our best, it is easy to do things half-heartedly or procrastinate on what we should take care of right now. In the long run, that leads to problems.

It is easy to think that sleep is not important, especially when you are younger. The problem is that energy does run low even for the young. Then people turn to energy drinks that are not healthy. When insomnia occurs, many pick up their phones to kill time. This is turning to the root cause of the problem to solve the problem it is causing. Develop the habits of a healthy sleep routine. Between healthy eating, getting exercise, and getting the right amount of sleep, you can operate at a more successful level. There is no need to sabotage yourself by choosing poorly when it comes to these areas. You have control over them.

······

## 31

## GIVE YOUR BEST

And let us not grow weary of doing good, for in due season we will reap, if we do not give up.

Galatians 6:9

What you put out into the world matters. Your level of effort is noticed and becomes what you will be known for by others. If you put out sloppy, careless work, you get a reputation for being someone who does not care. If you put out work that has effort and care, you become known as a conscientious person. Others put more trust in conscientious people. I know I put important matters into the hands of people who have shown me they will apply effort, care, and attention.

Most leaders do not want people on their teams they know they will have to go behind to clean up messes, fix mistakes, or complete the job fully. If they have to do all that themselves, why do they need that team member?

Giving your best is about building up the character trait of integrity. Integrity is doing what you said you would do, in the manner in which you said you would do it, and by the time you said you would do it. It is about fulfilling a promise and making the effort to do it right.

·⋯•••·•••⋯·

# 32

## GO TO CHURCH

> And let us consider how to stir up one another to love and good works, **25** not neglecting to meet together, as is the habit of some, but encouraging one another, and all the more as you see the Day drawing near.
>
> Hebrews 10:24-25

For many Christians, there can be the belief that there is no need to attend a church service. There are so many valid reasons to attend, however. We are called to worship God with other believers. It is stated in the bible in Hebrews, Acts, Corinthians, Colossians, and Romans to name a few books.

We become part of a community when we go to a church and become active within it. We meet other believers and we get the opportunity to serve. Being active within a community of believers will help to disciple us. We can find mentorship within this community to help us understand more of God's word.

We are not called to walk this life alone and certainly not in our faith walk. God will use the people within our faith community to help us in our times of need. We will hear words of encouragement and conviction when we need them most. In doing it alone, we miss out on that. The world can lead us astray. Staying closely connected with other believers will help us recognize what is right and true and what is not.

## 33

# GOOD STEWARDSHIP MATTERS

*As each has received a gift, use it to serve one another, as good stewards of God's varied grace*

1 Peter 4:10

How we carry out our duties when being entrusted with a resource shows the world our character. It goes back to being trustworthy. If you cannot be trusted with small things, you will not be given bigger things to manage. Simply taking care of what you have is a way to develop the habit of good stewardship. It demonstrates gratitude as well.

We have stewardship over many things. It can range from babysitting a younger sibling to owning your first car. You are the steward of that person at the time they are in your care and you are the steward of that car. Treating either badly is not stewardship. Will you neglect what is entrusted to you? Will you allow that child in your care to go without a meal or be in harm's way by wandering off unsupervised? Will you drive the car without ever getting an oil change or keeping it clean?

It comes down to our level of gratitude. We care about the things we are grateful to have. It is having the maturity to know that if you care for items properly, they can serve your needs longer. It is not expecting another person to replace things that you failed to take care of properly. However, it is also about our level of respect for others. When we borrow something, we return it in good condition and by the time we said we would. We do not misplace the item or let it get broken. How you care for the things in your charge shows the world if you can be trusted.

## 34

## GUARD YOUR THOUGHTS

Finally, brothers, whatever is true, whatever is honorable, whatever is just, whatever is pure, whatever is lovely, whatever is commendable, if there is any excellence, if there is anything worthy of praise, think about these things.

Philippians 4:8

What we think creates our reality. It does not make it a reality for others, just us. Once you understand the power of your thoughts, you will want to guard them. Our thinking can be faulty. That is human nature. We can generalize information, distort it, or delete it altogether.

This is why you can have several people in the exact same environment and situation, but they each report differences in what was seen, heard, and experienced. The person who filters everything through a negative lens will easily notice negative things while deleting positives.

When we generalize information, we can take past experiences and assume the same will happen in the future. We generalize the experience from one to the other. Distortions are when something is mistaken for that which it is not. Mind reading would be an example. When we make assumptions about what others are thinking, we are distorting things. We do not know, but we assign meaning to it anyway. For example, your friend does not text you back. You decide in your mind that she is giving you the silent treatment and that she is mad at you. You then feel bad. The lack of a returned text could be for many reasons, but you assigned this one without having any facts.

When we guard our thoughts, we avoid letting them run wild and jump to conclusions. We do not assume the worst in situations. We wait to get facts before we react. We make an intentional effort to find the good in a situation so that we do not train ourselves only to notice the bad. We guard our thoughts by what we allow to influence our thinking as well.

·····•••····

# 35

## HOLD YOUR GROUND

No temptation has overtaken you that is not common to man. God is faithful, and he will not let you be tempted beyond your ability, but with the temptation he will also provide the way of escape, that you may be able to endure it.

1 Corinthians 10:13

In order to hold your ground, you have to know your values. It is extremely difficult to hold your ground when you have no idea what you stand for. Life will present endless opportunities for you to compromise your beliefs when you do not hold your ground.

Setting good boundaries with others helps prevent being in situations where others may push you to compromise your beliefs. When we live in alignment with our values, our character will show through. That message will be loud and clear when we are consistent about it. If we are inconsistent, then others know you may just compromise after all.

Being wishy-washy about our values and beliefs, and not holding good boundaries, leaves the door wide open to temptations where we must make a choice. Do we cave and go with the crowd even though we do not feel good about it, or do we hold our ground to protect our integrity?

## 36

## INVEST IN YOURSELF

An intelligent heart acquires knowledge, and the ear of the wise seeks knowledge.

Proverbs 18:15

Now that you have graduated, please do not think this is the end of learning and growing. As the years go by, others may offer you the opportunity to participate in certification programs or other professional development courses. However, others may never offer this to you. So many people get frustrated that their employer does not offer training and development. Or they do not offer what the person wants to receive.

Please do not wait for others to invest in you. Invest in yourself. I realize that means you are the one who has to pay the bill and that is ok. You will never waste money when you spend it on developing yourself and gaining new skills. In fact, sometimes it is better that you are the one to pay the bill because you have skin in the game. When things are offered for free, people often do not see the value in it and begin to skip classes. When you have skin in the game, you show up. You want to get as much value out of the program as you can.

You are worth the time and the money to invest in your continued growth and development. It opens doors and keeps you from getting stagnant. You see additional opportunities for yourself and have the self-confidence to pursue them.

··•••••···

## 37

## KEEP BEING CURIOUS

> Ask, and it will be given to you; seek, and you will find; knock, and it will be opened to you.
>
> Matthew 7:7

Believe it or not, being curious helps you with problem-solving and being more at peace with challenges that arise. People who lack a sense of curiosity tend to avoid challenges and get very stressed with problems. They tend to lack problem-solving skills. They only focus on the problem and their feelings about how awful it is.

Curiosity keeps you engaged and seeking out an understanding of what is fully going on with the challenge. It keeps you asking questions about options that could lead to solutions. Curiosity also helps you feel more alive. You seek out an understanding of the world around you. When you are actively doing that, you are talking to others, reading, investigating, and contemplating new ideas. People who lack curiosity look at their world with a level of disinterest that keeps them from engaging actively in it. They tend to be bored and lack motivation. Curious people seek out new experiences. New experiences can lead to seeing new places, meeting new people, and having fun. That adds joy to your life.

We see curiosity being quite high in young children, but as we grow older, it begins to diminish. Sadly, that happens because others around us begin to suppress our curiosity. Schools do this by teaching you what to think and not how to think. Parents get tired of the one thousand questions their child is asking. No one means to suppress it. They just do not understand the value of being curious. Keep being curious.

## 38

## KEEP THINGS SIMPLE

For God is not a God of confusion but of peace. As in
all the churches of the saints,

1 Corinthians 14:33

It is amazing how we can complicate things and then get ourselves stuck. We pile on layers of confusion by overthinking things. We get stuck in so much detail that we lose sight of the big picture. Sometimes the best option is to understand the big picture and be aware of the details, but not get entrenched in the details to the point you cannot take action.

Sometimes what it takes is a simple pros and cons list. If the pros outweigh the cons, then that may simply be your answer. Sometimes it is simply taking the next step and not worrying about all the steps that follow it. Just do the one for now. That keeps it simple. You cannot do the future steps before you take the very next one anyway.

We can suffer from what is called analysis paralysis. We overthink to the point we get ourselves stuck. This is where having a mentor or a group of trusted advisors can help you. Sometimes we just need another person to help us keep it simple. They may have the clarity we do not have. We are too close to the issue, but they are not. They can see a more straightforward path to suggest.

## 39

# KNOW YOUR BOUNDARIES

> You set a boundary that they may not pass, so that they might not again cover the earth.
>
> Psalm 104:9

We teach people how to treat us. That means when you allow others to say and do things that you find offensive or hurtful, you are teaching them it is ok with you. When they believe it is ok with you, they will keep doing it. Allowing others to cross your boundaries leaves you feeling angry, used, hurt, overwhelmed, and afraid. You become afraid to tell others no. You feel angry at others for treating you poorly. You end up overwhelmed because you allow others to dump things on you that you do not have the time or interest to do.

Learn about you and what your boundaries need to be. Pay attention to how you feel after interactions with others. This will help you to learn what is acceptable to you and what is not. Practice setting your boundaries by letting others know that what they said to you was not acceptable. You can practice setting boundaries by saying no to requests you do not have the time or the interest in. No is a complete answer by the way. You do not need to qualify it any further, unless in a work situation. You may have a manager ask you to take on a task that you know you do not have the time for. In those cases, you need to have a discussion and explain that. However, you are still protecting boundaries when you do that. You now have the opportunity to receive additional assistance or to put other things on hold so that you can do what is being requested.

Protecting your boundaries leads to being at peace. It cuts down on a lot of drama too. Teach others how you want to be treated and what you will not tolerate.

·····•·•···

## 40

# KNOW YOUR NON-NEGOTIABLES

Those whom I love, I reprove and discipline, so be zealous and repent.

Revelation 3:19

As you go through life, you will need to identify what you consider to be your non-negotiables. These are the things that are not open for discussion or compromises on your part. This can be things such as not dating someone who does drugs or abuses alcohol. It can be not compromising on your values or beliefs to be in a relationship with another person.

Compromising what you consider a non-negotiable puts you on a slippery slope. Once you cave in on something as important as the non-negotiable, it will be very easy to stop holding your ground and allow others to cross your boundaries. You will leave yourself wide open to potential manipulation, or worse abuse. Situations will begin to appear in your life that you never intended. Knowing your non-negotiables will help you quickly learn who should and should not be in your life.

People who know their values, identify their non-negotiables, hold their ground, and teach others to respect their boundaries are in a healthy place. You may see these things as being all the same, but each is a more refined aspect of the bigger picture.

·····•··•·····

# 41

## KNOW YOUR VALUES

For where your treasure is, there will your heart be also.

Luke 12:34

As mentioned in the prior passage, this is another aspect of being in a healthy place and receiving the respect you deserve. The foundation for boundaries, identifying non-negotiables, and holding your ground is knowing what you value.

To begin to identify your values, simply start brainstorming a list of things that you care about or that you want to see present in your life. For example, love, family, creativity, friends, travel, purpose, achievement, community, inclusion, diversity, etc... Just keep going until you cannot add any more. To help you keep going, think of things that would be important to you in the areas of family/friends/significant others, career, personal growth, health (mental and physical), finances, and spirituality. Focusing on those areas, can help spark values to add to your list.

Group similar ones together and choose the one that you see in that group that would be the foundation. If it is missing, the others would not be able to be present either. That begins to help you identify core beliefs. From there, choose five core beliefs. Journal why they are important to you. Once you have a handle on values, you can be proactive about protecting them. You can then make decisions in life that honor them rather than compromise them.

## 42

### KNOWING THE ONE

> Do not be unequally yoked with unbelievers. For what partnership has righteousness with lawlessness? Or what fellowship has light with darkness?
>
> 2 Corinthians 6:14

This is a major subject! How do you know the right one to marry? Although there is a lot of advice on the subject, here is a suggestion for you. Evaluate what you want in your life. Consider those values once again. Consider your goals and your dreams. Write out specifically what you want in your future. Write out what characteristics you want in your future spouse.

As you write things out, consider the following details: how will you support each other's goals, what are the non-negotiables, what values you must have in common, do you want children, do you have a particular religious belief that your partner must share, how will you handle finances, how you will handle making big decisions, and so forth.

It is easy to be head over heels in love and not think about these details. One suggestion is to write all this out before you begin to seriously date anyone. Then as you begin dating, you can see if the person is going to match up to what you have identified as being important to you. Getting clear beforehand will help with discernment later. You may be dating someone you think is fantastic; however, if many points are a mismatch to what you have determined as important to you, then you have your answer. If you are dating someone you think is a good match, discuss what you wrote out with him or her. Hear what they have to say about these important points.

·····●··●····

# 43

## KNOW YOUR WHY

> But in your hearts honor Christ the Lord as holy, always being prepared to make a defense to anyone who asks you for a reason for the hope that is in you; yet do it with gentleness and respect,
>
> 1Peter 3:15

Anything you invest your time in deserves some consideration as to why you are doing it. As life gets busy, you will have to pick and choose how you spend your time. Knowing why you want to do something will help you to eliminate the things that ultimately do not serve you well.

There may be two things that appear worthwhile and it becomes hard to decide which to do. If you have set certain goals for yourself and you know why you want to achieve them, you can discern more easily which choice matches your why.

Knowing your why can help you persevere to achieve your goals when you want to call it quits. For example, you are pursuing a degree or an advanced degree. Knowing deep down why it matters to you that you achieve that can be the one thing you hang onto in the challenging moments. That why becomes a backup reservoir when your tank runs empty.

····•··•···

## 44

## LEARN ABOUT RESILIENCE

Rejoice in hope, be patient in tribulation, be constant in prayer.

Romans 12:12

Resilience is our ability to adapt, overcome, or recover from difficulties. Some have more resilience than others. Think about people who have had to overcome tremendous hardships and still tend to have a positive outlook on life. Those are people who have higher levels of resilience. Think about people who become unglued at the slightest bit of a challenge. Their resilience levels are low.

In my research for other books, I found that people who have higher levels of resilience tend to see problems as temporary rather than permanent. They also see the problems associated only with a particular situation and not their whole life generally. Those are two key differences that set apart those with resilience and those without.

Resilient people learn from life's challenges. They take what they learn and make the future better for themselves and others. Resilient people are hopeful too. There is always the belief that if they keep pursuing a solution, one will appear. There are books and programs that teach resilience. Invest in yourself to learn more about how you can increase your resilience. Life will sucker punch you at times. That is just a reality. How fast you get back up and how well you carry on will depend on your level of resilience.

## 45

## LEARN GOAL SETTING

And the Lord answered me: "Write the vision; make it plain on tablets, so he may run who reads it. For still the vision awaits its appointed time; it hastens to the end—it will not lie. If it seems slow, wait for it; it will surely come; it will not delay.

Habakkuk 2:2-3

Goal setting will help you move forward toward the things that matter most to you. People who talk about things, but never write them down in a goal format, are just sharing their dreams. Dreams are a beautiful thing. Achieving them is even more beautiful.

There are known formats for goal setting. One of the most popular is S.M.A.R.T. This stands for Specific, Measurable, Attainable, Relevant (or realistic), and Timeline. You have to be specific about what you want to achieve. For example, you want to read more books to increase your knowledge. To get specific, you can say you will read 24 books the next year. It is measurable because you can count two books per month. It is attainable because two books per month can fit into your schedule. It is relevant because the actions you are taking match what you are trying to accomplish. The timeline is one year.

Setting goals helps us be open to learning new skills, being open to new experiences, and pushing ourselves outside our comfort zone. Goal setting is a form of growth and helps us feel positive about ourselves and our life. Happier people are goal-setters and goal-getters. They are pursuing their dreams. Simply being in pursuit of the goal has great value because, with each forward step, there is a wonderful feeling of joy.

·····••·••···

# 46

## LEARN HOME BASICS

> And to aspire to live quietly, and to mind your own affairs, and to work with your hands, as we instructed you, so that you may walk properly before outsiders and be dependent on no one.
>
> 1 Thessalonians 4:11-12

Your school and home life so far may have led you to be so busy, that you have not had the chance to learn some of the things you will need to know once you are living on your own. I know that cooking and cleaning are not exciting topics. Car maintenance may feel overwhelming. However, knowing how to take care of some basic things on your own will be beneficial. Learning home basics will help you to save time and money in the long run. Your home life will feel organized and not overwhelming.

When I was with a nonprofit program, we had homeowners who needed sweat equity hours. I had one of the future homeowners help me clean a building for some of her sweat equity hours. I just assumed she knew how to mop a floor, so I left her with it. I came back to see her spreading a soapy film all over the place. She thought that more soap was a good thing. We had to go back and keep rinsing the floor with clear water to remove the excess soap. Another time, a relative of mine did not realize you could not put dish soap that is used for hand washing at the sink in her dishwasher. The kitchen was filled with soap bubbles coming out of the dishwasher.

Fortunately, we have YouTube. You can find just about any topic on there to teach you how to do something. You may still decide to have car maintenance done by the local garage. At least knowing the intervals at which you should change your oil, rotate the tires, and perform certain tune-ups is just as important. If you have no idea, you will be setting yourself up for bigger, costlier repairs because you did not do the smaller, affordable maintenance.

·····•·•···

# 47

## LEARN TO COMMUNICATE

> Know this, my beloved brothers: let every person be quick to hear, slow to speak, slow to anger;
>
> James 1:19

Effective communication will set you apart from others. If you have aspirations to advance in your career, communicating well with team members, superiors, and customers is one way to help others see the value you add.

There are countless examples I could give you from work situations where ineffective communication led to extra work, delays, mistakes needing to be corrected, or confusion. That all leads to frustration. You can never assume others know what you mean. In reality, there is what you thought you said, what you actually said, what you thought others heard, and what they actually heard.

Simply sticking to the basics of answering the who, what, when, where, why, and how questions, will help you to cover your bases. Leaving those details out creates problems for others. People are not mind-readers and you must fill in the gaps in the information. Too often assumptions are made about what was thought to be communicated or understood. Ask for others to help you know if you are communicating well. Ask them what they understood from the information you shared. You will very quickly realize what gaps exist.

··••·•···

## 48

## LEARN TO FORGIVE

But if you do not forgive others their trespasses, neither will your Father forgive your trespasses.

Matthew 6:15

Everyone gets hurt at some point in their life. We cannot escape that. However, how you deal with hurt will determine the quality of your life. Hurt that is not managed grows into resentment. Carrying resentment around is like drinking poison and waiting for the other person to die. You will be the one who will suffer for your lack of forgiveness.

I will not say this is easy. It is not. It takes work on a daily basis, especially if the hurt is a significant one. Some situations are very heavy duty and may take years to reach a place of forgiveness. The gift of forgiveness is for you and only you. Just like resentment becomes your poison, forgiveness becomes your gift of peace. You benefit from it.

It has nothing more to do with the person who wronged you. You are not giving them anything. You are giving yourself the freedom to move past anger and resentment. You are giving yourself the freedom to move toward healing, peace, and joy.

This other person lives rent-free in your head when you refuse to forgive. Forgiveness is not saying what he or she did was acceptable in any way. You choose to lay down the power that their hurtful behavior has had over you. They do not get to take anything more from you that you do not give. It is up to you if you will continue to give them your peace and joy or if you will claim it for yourself.

## 49

## LEARN TO INFLUENCE

Give instruction to a wise man, and he will be still wiser; teach a righteous man, and he will increase in learning.

Proverbs 9:9

My mentor John C. Maxwell has always said that leadership is influence, nothing more, nothing less. There are many with titles that indicate being in charge and leading, but if they do not influence others, they are not leaders. You cannot lead if no one is following you.

To influence, you have to have integrity first and foremost. Being a person of character is one of the most powerful ways to have influence. When a highly respected person speaks, people tend to listen. Influential people care about others and spend time building relationships. They nurture these relationships and support others. On a team, the person who does this is usually the one who truly leads the way. The team looks to this person for their input on how to proceed. So, you can be a leader without a title.

While you are waiting to be recognized and promoted in your career, you can focus on being a leader through your influence. This is especially true if you are just starting in your career. How can you influence things for the better in your immediate environment?

# 50

## LET GOD LEAD

Trust in the Lord with all your heart, and do not lean on your own understanding. In all your ways acknowledge him, and he will make straight your paths.

Proverbs 3:5-6

It is easy to get in the driver's seat and think you know the way better than God does. Christians will always say to let God lead, but in truth, how often do we get in the driver's seat and push forward with what we think is best?

We are human and fail to follow through on what we speak to each other on Sundays. Come Monday, we think we know what we need to do and push forward. We forget that we need to rely on God at all times. We need to pray and pause. We have to give time to recognize when God is answering our prayers. If we pray and rush ahead without paying attention to what God is showing us, then who is in the driver's seat? God already has the perfect answer and the plan is perfectly worked out. We just need to get out of the way and let Him lead us.

It has taken me most of my life to learn this one. I now pray and pause. I stop and listen. I look for the messages God will send to me to help me choose better. He knows what is on my heart and all the internal debates I have going on. I pray for clarity and wisdom. Letting God stay in the driver's seat means your journey will have his hand on all that you do. You will be blessed and you will be on the right path.

·····•·•····

# 51

## LIMIT CREDIT CARDS

The rich rules over the poor, and the borrower is the slave of the lender.

Proverbs 22:7

Consumer debt is at an all-time high. Families are struggling to pay the monthly minimum because the interest rate is so high on those cards. They live paycheck to paycheck doing it. It is going to take many years to pay it off as well.

There are many reasons why some have high debt on credit cards. Sometimes it is due to medical bills and being short on cash to buy other necessities. It could also be because of impatience. Credit cards let you have that new, shiny object right now instead of having to wait to save the cash for it. Jealousy can be another reason. If you are trying to buy things you see others have that you cannot afford, it is because you have not dealt with jealousy. Another deeper reason for this kind of debt is the issue of self-worth.

Low self-worth leads to buying designer-label items to feel good enough. It leads to shopping sprees when feeling a little down and wanting to feel better. Work on your emotional state first so that you do not go into debt for things that will not fix anything long-term.

## 52

## LIVE BELOW MEANS

Precious treasure and oil are in a wise man's dwelling,
but a foolish man devours it.

Proverbs 21:20

Learning to live below your means allows you to save for the future. It also allows you to think twice about what you need and what is possibly wasteful. What you do have, you have gratitude for it and are a good steward of it. Our world pushes excess. It pushes everyone to spend, spend, spend. It rarely talks about saving. It certainly does not talk about the benefits of living below your means.

I came across a story about a very wealthy family. The dad was a CEO of a company and had earnings most will only ever dream about. He traveled the world. However, one trip was highly influential. He saw poverty as he had never seen before. He saw people without shelter. He came home and told his family that they would begin to live on half his salary. He planned to save the rest for starting a non-profit program to serve those suffering greatly. They sold the huge house and cut back on spending drastically.

Years later, the family became closer to each other, they did not miss all the stuff from which they had downsized and embraced the mission the father presented to them. If we each lived below our means, we would then have the financial means to make an impact where we felt called to help.

··•••·•••··

# 53

## LIVE BY FAITH

For we walk by faith, not by sight

2 Corinthians 5:7

Most of us would say we live by faith. We are believers and trust in God's promises. However, we often do things that demonstrate a lack of faith despite the words we say. Take Abraham for example. He tried to help God keep his promise by having a child with another woman. His age was quite advanced and somewhere deep down he did not believe the promise made to him would be seen in his lifetime. God did keep his promise and Sara had a son after Abraham already took things upon himself.

When we live by faith, we have to resist the temptation to hurry things along by taking things into our own hands. God is known by his character and he has already told us his promises. The promises will be kept. They will be kept according to God's perfect timing and not ours.

We will feel the nudge from God to go where we do not know where we are going. He will guide our way, showing us what we need to see when the time is right. God is the perfect trail guide! Living by faith is surrendering and trusting at a level many non-believers will not understand.

·····••·••···

## 54

## LIVE IN BALANCE

No one can serve two masters, for either he will hate the one and love the other, or he will be devoted to the one and despise the other. You cannot serve God and money.

Matthew 6:24

We live in exciting times. There are so many opportunities all around us. Technology is the most advanced it has ever been thus far. It can do amazing things for us. The pace of the world is speeding up as well. Things move very quickly and if we do not act quickly, we might miss out. That is a really big challenge for many of us. Fear of Missing Out (FOMO).

Because of FOMO, we try to put too much into each day. There is also another classical phrase, Carpe Diem, Seize the Day. I used to try to do too much each day and would neglect certain areas of my life because of it. Eating healthy would usually be the first thing to get dropped. I would live a grab-and-go lifestyle. I would sacrifice sleep too. That moved into fully sacrificing self-care. I was living life out of balance.

I learned a new phrase called Joy of Missing Out (JOMO). As I became wiser about what was worth my time and effort, I gladly missed out on things that did not add any value to life. I learned what my values were and put things to the test against those. Here is a simple phrase to remember. *If it does not align, then you need to decline.* You cannot live in balance keeping family, mental health, physical health, spiritual well-being, and personal enjoyment as priorities if you are saying yes to everything because of FOMO.

··•••••··

## 55

# MAKE YOUR BED

> Through sloth the roof sinks in, and through indolence the house leaks.
>
> Ecclesiastes 10:18

This is not exactly about keeping a clean home. It is deeper than that. It is about having some daily discipline that will serve you well in life. Successful people develop daily habits that help them achieve their goals. Having a schedule is one. Planning the night before helps keep the next morning from being a chaotic start to your day.

Having a daily routine of getting up early enough to exercise, reading from an inspirational book, choosing healthy foods to take with you to work, tidying up the house, and then leaving with plenty of time for traffic sets you up for a successful day. Those who hit snooze repeatedly, jump out of bed in a panic because they are late, and never make their bed. On those days, it never fails that the car keys cannot be found either.

The military has everyone make their beds before the day starts. It is part of having the mindset of being organized, intentional, and disciplined. It helps break the lazy habit. There is time in your schedule to tidy up your living space, get exercise, invest in your growth by reading good books, and work on your goals, all while working and having fun with friends. It can be done. Making your bed is a real task that needs to be done, but it is a metaphor for being intentional about daily disciplines that set you up for success.

····•·•····

## 56

## MANAGE YOUR PERSPECTIVE

We destroy arguments and every lofty opinion raised against the knowledge of God, and take every thought captive to obey Christ,

2 Corinthians 10:5

Learn to keep things in perspective. It is very easy to magnify problems bigger than what they really are. If left to our imagination, we can take a small thing and blow it up to be a major situation if not careful.

Get insights from trusted family and friends. Choose wisely though. Choose the people you see regularly working to keep things in perspective and not create drama in their lives with overreactions. Asking for input can give you other points of view that help you from blowing things out of proportion. This may be something you need to practice daily to short-circuit automatic panic reactions. Step back and breathe. Simply pausing can slow down the automatic reactions.

When we keep things in perspective, we are more likely to see solutions and reduce our stress. When we overreact, we spin our wheels in a state of panic and keep asking what we are going to do. We do not see options when in a panic. In relationships, if we keep things in perspective, we do not create additional problems that never existed in the first place. Step back and breathe. Choose to keep calm and keep things in perspective.

## 57

## MANAGE YOUR STRESS

> Humble yourselves, therefore, under the mighty hand of God so that at the proper time he may exalt you, casting all your anxieties on him, because he cares for you.
>
> 1 Peter 5:6-7

Life is going to get stressful. I am sure you have already experienced stress getting ready for finals week at school, or getting large projects completed by their deadlines. How well you manage your stress will matter as time goes on. Short term, you may think it is no big deal. Stress has cumulative effects on our bodies and those effects are harmful.

Unmanaged stress eventually grows into having a myriad of biological consequences on our cardiovascular systems, endocrine systems, and digestive systems. It affects our hair and skin. It leads to mental and emotional consequences too. Our fight-or-flight response system can become dysregulated and we begin to live with higher-than-normal levels of cortisol. That is what leads to other biological consequences.

Our brains do not know the difference between a deadline at the office and a real-life threat. We need to learn about stress management techniques and use them. There is a lot of research to back up the importance of stress management. Develop the habit early in life for reducing stress so you do not suffer the consequences later in life.

# 58

## NEVER TOLERATE DISRESPECT

Take no part in the unfruitful works of darkness, but instead expose them.

Ephesians 5:11

As stated earlier, we teach others how to treat us. Setting good boundaries and maintaining them shows others we will not tolerate being disrespected. I want to go a step further on this topic. It is also about the people we spend time with and their disrespecting others too.

While you do not have control over your friends and family members, speaking up about disrespectful treatment with each other helps to improve relationships. It reduces fighting within the family or group of friends. Also, if out with family or friends, do not tolerate them being rude and disrespectful to the staff at restaurants, stores, hotels, or other customer service situations.

If you silently condone the disrespect, they will think you are okay with it, even if you are not. The world is full of people who are quick to disrespect others. Be different and set the expectations that if you are present, you do not engage in that kind of behavior.

··•••••···

## 59

# No More Drama

*But now you must put them all away: anger, wrath, malice, slander, and obscene talk from your mouth*

Colossians 3:8

People love drama! They may say they do not, but when they engage in gossip, betray the trust of another by sharing information told to them in confidence, or trash talk another, they most certainly do. Blaming others for their mistakes to correct is another form of drama.

Drama-prone people are attention seekers. They love to be the center of attention sharing a juicy story or playing the victim claiming others are at fault. People who avoid drama do not gossip or carry information shared with them to others. When gossiping starts up, they walk away. If there is a real conflict between one person and another, the person will work to resolve the issue without blaming or trash-talking the other.

Drama escalates conflicts. Years ago, there were talk shows that stirred up conflict between people until they behaved in completely inappropriate ways. We still see this with reality tv shows. The people on these shows are not role models. Our society has changed over time and acting outrageously due to escalated drama seems to be an everyday occurrence. If everyone chose to be respectful and eliminate the drama, many of the conflicts would cease. We live in peace when we choose no more drama.

## 60

## OFFER SOME HELP

In all things I have shown you that by working hard in this way we must help the weak and remember the words of the Lord Jesus, how he himself said, 'It is more blessed to give than to receive.'

Acts 20:35

There will always be the opportunity to serve others in life. There will always be situations where help is needed. While you cannot say yes to everything that is requested of you, work to find time to help when you can.

The benefits of volunteering and serving others have been studied. It has been shown to reduce stress and lead to positive feelings. We can find a sense of meaning and purpose when we serve an organization that has a mission we believe in. We can learn new skills through this as well. Additionally, it is a great way to expand your network. Previously it was mentioned about developing social capital and building your circle.

As you engage in serving your community, you will see ways in which you add value. You may have never thought about what you bring to the table, but you bring your unique value to situations. Go volunteer and find purpose, increase your sense of well-being, add new skills, and grow your network. It is a win-win for everyone.

···•·•··

# 61

## ORGANIZE YOUR DOCUMENTS

*But all things should be done decently and in order.*

1 Corinthians 14:40

You will thank yourself for this one every time you apply for a new job or require a copy of your birth certificate. Having worked in Human Resources, I was always surprised by the number of people who had to find their documents or apply for replacements. Even though we are in a digital world, some items must be presented in the original paper form for validity.

Your vital documents are just that-vital. Treat them as such. You will want to get your documents in order as you graduate. You are going to need them in more situations than you realize. Additionally, you want to keep them in a safe place, but where they are easily found only by you. That is your identity.

As you go through your career, you will need your school transcripts as well. Keep those with your other vital documents so that you have what you need right when a new opportunity presents itself. So many people miss out on deadlines and opportunities because of not having the documents they need when they need them.

# 62

## Own Your Mistakes

> Whoever conceals his transgressions will not prosper, but he who confesses and forsakes them will obtain mercy
>
> Proverbs 28:13

If we never accept responsibility for our mistakes, how we will ever grow? We grow because of the lessons learned from our mistakes. No one goes through life perfectly. It is ok to fail because failing propels us forward.

We gain vital insights when we own our mistakes, review what went wrong, and develop strategies to prevent them in the future. Wisdom is developed going through that process. They say that experience is the best teacher, but it is evaluated experience that is the best teacher. If we do not take the time to review and understand our experiences, we cannot learn from them.

Sometimes it will be embarrassing to admit our mistakes, but we can get over that. People respect those who own their mistakes and work to correct them. Those who cast blame everywhere else are not respected and certainly not trusted. Owning our mistakes is a character-building experience.

# 63

## PLAN TO SUCCEED

*For which of you, desiring to build a tower, does not first sit down and count the cost, whether he has enough to complete it?*

Luke 14:28

You may have heard the phrase "Fail to plan, plan to fail". What it means is if we do not take the time to think about what it is we want to accomplish and develop some action steps to reach it, we will not achieve it. We set ourselves up for failure by not planning.

Planning means getting clear on what it is you want to accomplish. If you have only a vague idea, it will be hard to know what actions you need to take. If you are clear on what you want to accomplish but do not identify what might be some appropriate action steps, chances are you will not take any action. Plans do not have to be complicated to be successful. In fact, keeping things simple is a good approach.

The lack of a plan is what will be your biggest obstacle to having what you want in life. Drifting along without one is leaving things to chance. Maybe you will get lucky here and there, but if you truly want to craft the life that you want, it is going to require a plan.

·····●·●·●····

# 64

## Plan To Tithe

Bring the full tithe into the storehouse, that there may be food in my house. And thereby put me to the test, says the Lord of hosts, if I will not open the windows of heaven for you and pour down for you a blessing until there is no more need.

Malachi 3:10

When we tithe, we are showing God we are giving him the best of our resources right off the top. He is not getting what we have left over. By creating a budget to allow you to tithe, you are showing good stewardship over what he has provided to you.

Additionally, stepping out in faith to give the full tithe also shows God that you trust him. He tells us in the bible he will provide for us. Tithing teaches us to recognize God as our sole provider and that all we have belongs to him.

We grow in our character when we tithe. We are taught it is better to give than to receive. Tithing allows us to give to others first. We are less likely to buy material items that have only a fleeting moment of happiness. Tithing can allow us to sow seeds into others who need help. The joy we get from that is deeper and longer lasting. We learn to live in balance when we create budgets, we are good stewards of what we have, and we give freely by tithing.

····•··•····

## 65

## PRIORITIZE NOT MULTITASK

But seek first the kingdom of God and his righteousness, and all these things will be added to you.

Matthew 6:33

Our world pulls us in so many directions. On the job, being seen as a multi-tasker is a good thing. However, how well do we really do on tasks that have to compete for our attention? The number of errors rises the more we attempt to multitask. Also, the amount of time it takes to complete several multi-tasked items is longer than just doing each task one at a time until completed.

Bouncing from one thing to another, and leaving tasks in various states of incompletion, is chaotic. It adds to our stress levels too. It is better to look at all the tasks and prioritize them based on importance and urgency. Also, if time is limited, you can apply the 80/20 rule. That rule states that 20 percent of the tasks have 80 percent of the impact. So, focus on those items first and complete them before moving to the next.

If you have more than one project due and they are of equal importance and have similar deadlines, establish the tasks for each that must be done that day. Only do those. You will still feel that sense of orderliness and completion because what was scheduled for that day was finished.

··•••••···

## 66

## PROGRESS NOT PERFECTION

> Not that I have already obtained this or am already perfect, but I press on to make it my own, because Christ Jesus has made me his own. Brothers, I do not consider that I have made it my own. But one thing I do: forgetting what lies behind and straining forward to what lies ahead, I press on toward the goal for the prize of the upward call of God in Christ Jesus.
>
> Philippians 3:12-14

This a favorite phrase of mine. It permits us to just move forward. We do not have to get anything perfect. We will not do anything perfectly. We are human. Often, people get stuck in the process of growth because they did not get things just right.

The truth is, we often learn more when things are not going perfectly right. Life will throw us curveballs and how well we adjust to those increases our resilience. The important thing is that we keep moving forward and not letting perfectionism stop us dead in our tracks. There is a mindset that can trap us and it is called "All or Nothing". It tells us that we must do all things just right or we should not even start at all.

The "All or Nothing" mindset is the opposite of the "Progress Not Perfection" mindset. If you are telling yourself all the reasons why you should not even get started on taking action toward a goal, then you are stuck in the All or Nothing mindset. It is better to get started and then determine your next step rather than not start at all.

## 67

## READ GOOD BOOKS

All Scripture is breathed out by God and profitable for teaching, for reproof, for correction, and for training in righteousness,

2 Timothy 3:16

We are so fortunate to live in a time when we have access to so many resources. Incorporate the habit of reading books that show you new ways to think about your world, learn new skills, and develop a growth plan. It is shown that those who are successful generally are readers. Many I know read a book a week. In a mentorship group I belong to, they frequently say "Leaders are Readers".

Reading helps keep the mind sharper too. Studies have shown that those who read are exercising more of the gray matter in their brain and that is linked to reduced chances of having Alzheimer's disease.

Reading has many benefits from learning new information, increasing focus and memory, and also reducing stress.

Now I realize some of you may not enjoy reading. You can always listen to audiobooks and do other things to exercise your gray matter such as doing challenging puzzles. Again, we live in a time where we have access to many resources and also many options for how we choose to access information. Do not become stagnant. Keep reading!

·····•··•····

# 68

## RELEASE DEAD WEIGHT

Set your minds on things that are above, not on things that are on earth

Colossians 3:2

This is about releasing what no longer serves you. It is about removing the clutter from your life. Clutter is what takes up space, time, and energy, but does not give you anything in return. Clutter comes in many forms. It is not always objects. It can be social activities and relationships too.

If an item truly gives you joy, keep it. If you are having to move the item out of your way over and over without feeling any joy for it, then it needs to move on. It needs to clear the way for something that does bring you joy. The same is true for groups you may have joined. In the beginning, the group served a purpose in your life and you got in return as much or more as you put in. However, if you put more in now than you get in return, is it worth your time and energy? It may be time to say goodbye.

Additionally, you may have friend acquaintances who take more than they give. Consider what you could be doing instead of spending time with people you do not enjoy. Things come and go in life. Not everything is meant to be permanent. Once it has served its purpose, it is ok to express gratitude for what it gave, but then let go. Say goodbye.

··· • •• • •• ···

# 69

## SAVE SOME MONEY

On the first day of every week, each of you is to put something aside and store it up, as he may prosper, so that there will be no collecting when I come.

1 Corinthians 16:2

This is closely related to the prior topic on living below your means. Part of budgeting is to help make sure you have money saved for important occasions or emergencies. Life will throw you curveballs and having money saved will help you get through those times with less stress. No one wants to pay for house or car repairs, but eventually, it is required.

When you have the habit of saving some of your paychecks each time, you can not only deal with the repair situations, but you will also have money left to still go do the things that mean something to you. All of us have dreams, but those who never save money to take action on their dreams, never get to see any of them come true.

If you begin the habit while you are young to save money, you will be amazed at what can happen with it if you also invest some of it. Then be patient and do not touch it. Later, when you need it, the funds will be there in an amount that will be more than enough to cover you. Society tells us to keep up with the Joneses and max out our credit cards. However, wise people do not do that and they save.

## 70

## SPECIALIZE IN SOMETHING

And he has filled him with the Spirit of God, with skill, with intelligence, with knowledge, and with all craftsmanship,

Exodus 35:31

When we are young, we often have many interests. That is a good thing. Take some time to try out various interests to learn more about what you love and what you do not. This helps you to begin to zero in on some areas that speak to your heart and your passion. Earlier it was written about finding your passion. Once you find your passion, begin to specialize in it.

We have many who are generalists in our world and there is great value in that. It helps you be more flexible in finding a new job. When you specialize, you stand apart from the generalists. You are now becoming someone who offers a specific value in a specific field. This can be a very lucrative position to be in.

Our world needs those who excel in their gifts and offer those gifts in a way that solves problems. The world will always have problems. If you can be someone who specializes in offering a solution to a particular problem, you can be of great service to those who need it.

··•••·•••··

# 71

## Time is Valuable

> Yet you do not know what tomorrow will bring. What is your life? For you are a mist that appears for a little time and then vanishes.
>
> James 4:14

Time is the one thing we spend each day and it cannot be replaced. Think about that for a minute. You can spend money and go earn more to replace it. When you spend time, that is it. It is forever gone. When we are young, we think we have all the time in the world, so we do not worry about how we spend it.

As we get older, and especially after we have children of our own, we begin to see just how precious time is. It does go by faster and faster as we age. We all get the same twenty-four hours in a day. Some of us use it better than others. Some plan their time to make the most effective use of what they have. Others waste it in front of a video game or the tv. Now, there is nothing wrong with downtime and enjoying a game with friends. However, if personal dreams and goals start getting put aside because you cannot find the time to work on them, then is it worth your time?

Being mindful of your time matters. Once you have your priorities and values aligned, you will quickly see where requests for your time do not align and you need to decline. Why spend time on something that has no value? Time is a precious commodity and needs to be spent on what matters.

# 72

## Travel the World

And I heard the voice of the Lord saying, "Whom shall I send, and who will go for us?" Then I said, "Here I am! Send me."

Isaiah 6:8

If you get the chance to travel and see other countries, please take the trip. You will have the opportunity to understand different cultures, learn their history, see their architecture, and try their foods. When we stay stuck only in our familiar surroundings, we lose out on expanding our experiences in life. We grow when we are put into new situations. We learn to adapt to differences when we travel.

When we travel, we quickly see how convenient things are in the world we come from and are put to the test when we have to get along in a new country. We may have to rely on hand gestures to be understood.

We may have to be patient as we figure out public transportation. We may make new friends because someone comes along to help us.

Traveling is the gateway to expanding your world within your heart and your mind. You will come to appreciate the beauty of other cultures and the people you meet. You will learn about other points of view and forever be changed once you understand another perspective on a global issue. Traveling gets us out of our comfort zone and grows us in ways we cannot imagine.

# 73

## TRUST YOUR GUT

Beloved, do not believe every spirit, but test the spirits to see whether they are from God, for many false prophets have gone out into the world.

1 John 4:1

We were all given a gut instinct for a reason. There have been numerous occasions when trusting my gut served me well. If something just does not feel right, then something probably is not right. Our gut instinct has been studied by some scientists as well. They found that the gut has a nervous system of its own and produces chemicals just like the brain does when thinking.

It is easy to talk ourselves out of our gut feeling when our gut is telling us to do something that our brain says is not logical. Our brains will talk us out of taking a leap of faith. It will tell us everything that will go wrong and not what will go right.

One thing you can do when you are caught in the battle between your brain and your gut feeling is to list out all the things that can go right and all that can go wrong. For what can go wrong, can you find ways to overcome them? Can you live with the consequences if things go wrong? Can those consequences be redirected into something that gets you back on track? Are all the things that can go wrong even realistic? If your gut feeling is strong, you have many reasons to believe what can go right and have plans for addressing what might go wrong, then go for it. Trust your gut.

## 74

## YOU ARE ENOUGH

> So then you are no longer strangers and aliens, but you are fellow citizens with the saints and members of the household of God,

Ephesians 2:19

This is a tough one for many. It is a challenge in this world with social media showing us unrealistic images of what is considered beautiful and successful. Social media is carefully crafted. The number of followers and likes a person gets becomes the gauge of their happiness.

Please know that you are enough. You are good enough. You are smart enough. You are pretty enough or handsome enough. You have been born with your unique gifts and talents. Instead of focusing on how you are not like someone else, focus on developing your gifts instead. Comparison is the thief of joy. Oftentimes, we compare ourselves to others who may have been developing their gifts longer than we have. Is that a fair assessment of you?

If you focus on your dreams, your gifts, your purpose, and your values; you will find you are a unique combination that no one can compare to you. You are one of a kind. You will always be enough for what you want in this life. Avoid chasing what others are doing just because it appears that is what everyone should be doing. Go after what fits you and only you. You are already enough for what you want to do in life.

····•··•····

## 75

## YOU DESERVE BETTER

Do not give dogs what is holy, and do not throw your pearls before pigs, lest they trample them underfoot and turn to attack you.

Matthew 7:6

As we go through life, it can be easy to settle for less than what we deserve. We either tell ourselves we are not worthy of better or that it is easier to not rock the boat. We stay in situations long past the time they are good for us with this kind of thinking.

If you find yourself in situations where you are not valued, it is time to leave. This can be in a job or a relationship. It could be in a volunteer situation or as a member of an organization. If you are not valued, then you deserve better.

You have to decide what you consider being treated as a person of value looks likes, sounds like, and feels like. Once you have that determined, see if your current situations treat you as such. If they do not, then you have to decide if you will stay or if you will go. There will always be new jobs, new organizations, and new relationships where you will be valued. Remember, you deserve better.

···•·•···

# ABOUT AUTHOR

Kelly Owens is the author of the book Death By Cubicle-Recovery From Burnout Without Quitting Your Job. She is also a contributing author to Volume 1 of Voices for Leadership. She has a Master's Degree in management and has had a variety of leadership roles in both for-profit and nonprofit organizations. She is a Certified Coach, Trainer, and Speaker with Maxwell Leadership. Additionally, she is a certified DISC Consultant and certified Master Practitioner of Neurolinguistic Programming.

In her free time, she enjoys time with her husband, their children, and grandchildren. Kelly also enjoys running, along with scuba diving with her husband in the Keys. They spend time riding around in their 1970 VW camper van. Her name is Janis and she is the model on the cover of this book.

Manufactured by Amazon.ca
Bolton, ON